Original title:

Leafen Drips Beneath the Dragon Hash

Author: Kätriin Kaldaru

ISBN HARDBACK: 978-1-80563-228-3

ISBN PAPERBACK: 978-1-80564-749-2

The Eruption of Celestial Calm

In twilight's glow, the stars ignite,
Their whispers dance in velvet night.
A moonbeam's touch, so soft and clear,
Awakens dreams we hold so dear.

With every pulse, the heavens sigh,
As constellations weave and fly.
A tapestry of light and grace,
In cosmic arms, we find our place.

Flares of color splash the sky,
While galaxies in silence cry.
The world's edge fades, we lose our mind,
In moments pure, our souls unwind.

Yet through the calm, a tempest stirs,
A swirling dance of stars' soft whirs.
In paradox of night and day,
We seek the truth, we find our way.

So let the night embrace our plight,
As wonders bloom in shades of light.
For in the dark, we find the spark,
That guides us home—that steals the dark.

Spheres of Stardust in the Canopy

Underneath the whispering trees,
Spheres of stardust drift on breeze.
They twinkle softly, hues collide,
In shadowed glens, where secrets hide.

A canopy of emerald dreams,
Where moonlit laughter gently beams.
Each branch a bridge to worlds untold,
Where stories weave in silver bold.

The nightingale sings songs of yore,
While pixies play and shadows soar.
With every flicker, spirits rise,
Embracing life beneath the skies.

Spheres aligned in cosmic dance,
A fleeting glimpse, a fleeting chance.
To capture moments draped in light,
To feel the magic of the night.

In this stillness, hearts entwined,
In celestial embrace, we're blind.
For stardust keeps our dreams in sway,
As dawn awaits to steal away.

Veins of Gold in Shattered Branches

In a hollow trunk where whispers dwell,
Golden veins in wood do swell,
An echo speaks of ancient lore,
Of time and tales, forevermore.

Beneath the boughs where sunlight threads,
A story thrives where hope still spreads,
Shattered branches cradle dreams,
In their embrace, the magic gleams.

The forest knows of hearts entwined,
Of lovers lost and souls aligned,
A tapestry of fate unwound,
In nature's grasp, their echoes sound.

From every leaf, a secret springs,
In rustling winds, the laughter rings,
Veins of gold in splintered wood,
Tell of days both dark and good.

Here linger shades of lives once bright,
Their flicker dances in the night,
In this enchanted realm so bold,
Veins of gold in stories told.

The Blossom of Forgotten Legends

In gardens rich where memories sleep,
Blossoms bloom, their colors deep,
Legends whisper on fragrant air,
Tales of bravery, of love laid bare.

Beneath the moon, soft shadows play,
Nurtured roots from yesterday,
In petals curled, the stories weave,
Of worlds once lived, and those who grieve.

Each bud a promise, sweetly borne,
Of heroes clad in courage worn,
Forgotten now, yet still they gleam,
In twilight's glow, they live, they dream.

The breeze carries their silent call,
To every heart, to one and all,
In every bloom, a spark ignites,
The blossom of ancient, starry nights.

So pause awhile, beneath the trees,
And let the legends ride the breeze,
In every bloom, a narrative grows,
Of tales untold, in soft repose.

Whirling Dervishes of the Forest

The forest spins, a vibrant dance,
With whirling leaves that take a chance,
In rustling skirts, the branches twirl,
Nature's rhythm, wild and unfurled.

Dervishes of the ancient wood,
In spirals of joy, they understood,
The secrets hidden in their flight,
As shadows twist in flickering light.

In circles wide, they spin and sway,
Chasing dreams that drift away,
Each whirl a story, each twirl a song,
In harmony, where souls belong.

With every turn, the earth does sigh,
A melody of night and sky,
In swirling forms, they cast a spell,
Whirling dervishes weave their tale well.

Embrace the dance, let spirits rise,
In nature's grasp beneath vast skies,
Join the carousel of light and lore,
Where whirling dervishes forever soar.

A Tapestry of Shadows and Stars

In twilight's glow, where shadows play,
A tapestry of light, it lays,
Stars entwined in velvet night,
Weaving dreams in silver light.

Each thread a whisper of the past,
In cosmic dance, their shadows cast,
Stories writ in brilliant hues,
Of ancient realms and faded views.

The moon, a weaver of the dark,
Seeks out the dreams that leave a mark,
Each heartbeat echoes, soft and keen,
In every stitch, a world unseen.

Beneath the sky, where silence hums,
The tapestry of night becomes,
A canvas bright, of life reborn,
In shadows cast, a new day's dawn.

So gaze upon the starlit sea,
Embrace the night, let spirits free,
For in the dark, the dreams ignite,
A tapestry of shadows, stars, and light.

Flames of Passion in the Dappled Light

In the forest, shadows twirl,
Where light and dark begin to swirl.
A fire ignites in gentle grace,
Passion's dance, in this hidden place.

Among the leaves, a secret sigh,
The sun dips low, the stars comply.
Hearts aflame with whispered dreams,
In dappled light, where magic gleams.

Beneath the boughs, where wildflowers bloom,
Love finds a path, dispelling gloom.
With every heartbeat, whispers grow,
In nature's arms, two souls in flow.

Time bends softly, moments freeze,
As laughter tumbles through the trees.
An echo of joy, sweet balm to the night,
In the forest's embrace, all feels right.

So let the flames consume the air,
In dappled light, we shed our care.
Let passion guide our curious flight,
Through the whispers of the starry night.

Embracing Whispers of the Sylvan

In the grove where echoes sing,
Nature weaves a sacred ring.
Every leaf and branch a song,
In sylvan realms, where we belong.

The breeze carries a soft refrain,
A melody that soothes the brain.
Embracing whispers, sweet and low,
Through tangled roots, our spirits flow.

Moonlight spills on silver streams,
Crickets serenade our dreams.
Together lost in twilight's bliss,
Each gentle touch, a lover's kiss.

The old oak watches, wise and true,
Guarding secrets known to few.
With every heartbeat, we intertwine,
In sylvan shadows, our hearts align.

Beneath the stars, unbound we roam,
In embracing whispers, we find home.
Among the leaves, our spirits soar,
In the sylvan hush, we long for more.

The Soliloquy of Broken Branches

A crackling sound beneath my feet,
Echoes of time, a tale bittersweet.
Broken branches tell of loss,
Nature mourns its heavy cross.

Yet in the chaos, life prevails,
Among the remnants, hope exhales.
Through shattered wood, new sprouts emerge,
Life's insistence, a quiet surge.

Whispers linger in the air,
Voices of those who still care.
Each fracture holds a memory true,
Of days long gone, yet shining through.

The soliloquy of silent trees,
Bears witness to the passing breeze.
In every break, a story told,
Of strength and beauty that unfolds.

So heed the calls of the ancient wood,
For in brokenness, life's understood.
From shadows deep, new light will bloom,
The soliloquy of nature's room.

The Riddle of the Winding Thorns

In the thicket where secrets hide,
Winding thorns stand side by side.
A riddle spun in emerald green,
To those who dare, a mystery seen.

With every twist, the path discloses,
Waiting hearts, like blooming roses.
The game of fate, intricate and sly,
Will you dare to answer why?

Through tangled vines, our spirits yearn,
Lessons learned, yet still we burn.
Within the thorns, there lies a spark,
A brighter truth within the dark.

Yet tread with care, for beauty's guise,
Can cloak the sharp and cruel surprise.
The riddle calls, a chance to grow,
Past winding thorns, let courage flow.

So venture forth through bramble tight,
To unravel love's hidden light.
The riddle waits, your heart will guide,
Through winding paths, where dreams abide.

A Symphony of Rustling Silence

In the forest deep where shadows play,
Whispers of leaves begin to sway.
A gentle breeze wraps around,
Silent secrets without a sound.

Moonlight dances on the ground,
In the stillness, magic found.
Crickets sing a soft refrain,
Echoes of night, sweet and plain.

Nestled in the soft, warm earth,
Each rustle holds a tale of worth.
Stars above in silent guard,
Nature's beauty, quiet and hard.

With every sigh of trees at rest,
The world reveals its hidden zest.
In this symphony, hearts enthrall,
Rustling silence welcomes all.

Celestial Waters on Fallen Petals

Morning dew on petals glows,
Reflecting skies in soft repose.
Each drop a world, a tale untold,
In the light, pure magic unfolds.

Colors dance in gentle light,
A canvas spun from day to night.
Fallen petals, soft and wide,
Cradle dreams the winds confide.

Rippling waters catch the gleam,
A tranquil heart caught in a dream.
With every shimmer, truths arise,
Beneath the vast, enchanting skies.

Celestial realms in harmony,
Kissing earth with tender glee.
In each petal, worlds align,
Nature's grace, a love divine.

The Veil of Twilight's Embrace

When day bows low and shadows blend,
Twilight wraps the world, my friend.
A veil of dusk, so soft and sweet,
As stars begin their nightly greet.

Whispers linger in the air,
Dreams unfurl without a care.
Softly, softly, night descends,
Cloaked in wonder, time suspends.

Moonbeams bathe the earth in white,
Lending magic to the night.
Each breath a promise, still and clear,
In this twilight, love draws near.

The veil embraces all with grace,
Wrapping hearts in softest space.
In shadows deep, our spirits roam,
Finding solace, finding home.

Chasing Echoes Through Gnarled Wood

In the heart of woods so old,
Tree trunks twist like tales of gold.
Whispers echo through the air,
Secrets linger everywhere.

Branches weave a tapestry,
Rustling leaves invite the free.
Echoes chase the fading light,
Dancing shadows, taking flight.

Footfalls soft on earthy ground,
In the quiet, dreams abound.
Each turn leads to paths unknown,
In gnarled wood, our seeds are sown.

Nature sings a haunting tune,
Underneath the watchful moon.
Chasing echoes, hearts align,
In this wild, we find the divine.

Fables of the Falling Leaves

In autumn's breath, the whispers call,
Among the boughs, the leaves do fall.
Each hue a tale, of time that's passed,
A fleeting dance, a spell that's cast.

Crimson dreams on gentle ground,
In silence deep, they twirl around.
The winds will sing of days gone by,
As spirits soar beneath the sky.

Once vibrant green, now golden glow,
In nature's quilt, the stories flow.
Each rustle tells of life anew,
In fables spun, both old and true.

Celestial Flame and Verdant Glow

Beneath the stars, a fire ignites,
A flicker bright in waltzing nights.
Where shadows dance, and dreams take flight,
The cosmos speaks in colors bright.

Emerald leaves in twilight's embrace,
A sacred hush in a timeless space.
With every flick, the world transforms,
In whispers soft, a magic warms.

The moon, a pearl in night's vast sea,
Bears witness to our reverie.
In every spark, bright stories blend,
A dance of light that has no end.

Breath of Myth Amidst the Groves

In ancient woods where legends sleep,
The echoes of the past run deep.
Where fae and mortals softly tread,
With every step, a tale is spread.

The mossy floors, the twisted limbs,
Hold secrets sweet, where twilight dims.
In whispers soft, the breezes weave,
The timeless art of those who believe.

With every breath, a spirit sighs,
In harmony beneath the sky.
The trees converse in fate's soft rhyme,
A breath of myth that conquers time.

The Conductor of Leaves and Layers

In rustling halls, a maestro dwells,
With every breeze, the mystery swells.
He waves his arms, the leaves take flight,
In symphonies of day and night.

A dance of hues, in swirling grace,
Each layer tells its own embrace.
From twilight's hush to dawn's bright crown,
The world, a stage where dreams are sown.

With gentle hands, he spins the air,
Creating rhythms both wild and fair.
In nature's song, our hearts align,
A fleeting moment, so divine.

Beneath a Canopy of Secrets

Whispers dance in shaded glade,
Where shadows cling and memories fade.
The leaves they rustle, tales untold,
Of magic lost, and hearts of gold.

A gentle breeze, a breath of night,
It carries secrets, pure delight.
The stars above, they softly gleam,
As dreams entwine within a dream.

Beneath the boughs, where silence reigns,
A world of wonder still remains.
In every root, a story sown,
A tapestry of life unknown.

Each step we take, on trodden ground,
Echoes heard, though none around.
We tread the paths of lore and light,
Embracing shadows in the night.

Dreams Unfurl in Forest Depths

In tangled roots and dappled light,
Where dreams arise, hidden from sight.
The forest breathes, an ancient sigh,
Inviting souls to wonder, fly.

With every glance, the leaves unfold,
Revealing paths, both brave and bold.
A melody of rustling grace,
Calls forth a dance in nature's space.

Upon this ground where shadows creep,
The heart of woods begins to leap.
With wings of thought, the spirits soar,
In depths where time is lost, and more.

Each rustling branch, a beckoning hand,
To worlds unseen, where dreams withstand.
Through every twist, each winding trail,
The forest's song will never pale.

The Lament of Ancient Boughs

The ancient trees, they stand so tall,
With stories etched in bark, they call.
Their limbs extend, a sorrowed plea,
Of days gone by, of what can't be.

Each ring a year, each scar a tale,
In whispered winds, their voices wail.
Forgotten times, now lost in mist,
A yearning heart, a gentle tryst.

The echoes of a time once bright,
Are shadows cast in fading light.
Through storms and sun, they've borne the weight,
Of destinies entwined by fate.

In solitude, they stand and sigh,
For every song must say goodbye.
Yet in their roots, a strength remains,
The pulse of life, through joys and pains.

Glistening Tears of Autumn's Heart

When autumn paints the world in fire,
The leaves fall down, as hearts conspire.
With hues of gold and crimson bright,
They whisper tales of day and night.

Each falling leaf, a tear of grace,
In the wind's dance, they find their place.
A fleeting moment, beauty's gift,
As nature sighs, and spirits lift.

The chill of air, a tender kiss,
Reminds us all of what we miss.
In glistening drops, the sunlight gleams,
Awakening the faded dreams.

Through whispered woods, the stories flow,
Of seasons passed, of hearts that grow.
With every rustle, love will part,
These glistening tears of autumn's heart.

The Echoing Footsteps of Time

Whispers of ages long since passed,
Echo through corridors, shadows cast.
With each step taken, memories bloom,
In the silence, fate finds room.

Footprints dance on the dusty floor,
Tracing tales of those before.
The clock ticks softly in the night,
Guiding the lost toward the light.

Leaves rustle softly, secrets shared,
With every heartbeat, destiny dared.
Time, an enigma, slips like sand,
In its embrace, we understand.

Moments linger, threads entwined,
In this tapestry, we're all enshrined.
Echoes of laughter, tears now dry,
Trace the tales of those who fly.

So heed the whispers, the echoes call,
For with each footstep, we rise and fall.
In the twilight's glow, find your rhyme,
Embrace the journey, the echoing time.

Secrets of the Elder Spirits

In the depths of the ancient wood,
Elder spirits whisper, misunderstood.
Guardians of lore, in shadows they dwell,
Holding the secrets they dare not tell.

Moss-covered stones, silent and wise,
Witness to laughter beneath the skies.
A flickering lantern, the moon's soft glow,
Guides the way where few dare go.

Vines entwined in a lover's embrace,
Nature's allure, a magical place.
With each rustle, a story begins,
Of brave hearts and battles, of losses and wins.

Hidden beneath the thick, leafy crown,
The whispers of time never drown.
In the rust of the leaves, the soft breeze sings,
Of the mysteries held by these ancient kings.

So listen closely, to the tales they weave,
In the heart of the forest, take a reprieve.
For the elder spirits shall guide your way,
Unfolding the secrets of the day.

Enchantment Lingers in the Foliate

In the heart of the grove, magic resides,
Where every shadow, a secret hides.
Leaves shimmer bright with an emerald hue,
Holding enchantments both old and new.

Winds carry whispers, sweet and clear,
An orchestra played for those who hear.
Each rustling branch, a note divine,
Creating a spell that weaves through time.

Petals unfurl in the softest light,
Embracing the dawn, bidding goodbye to night.
Dewdrops glisten like jewels on skin,
Inviting the dreamers to venture within.

In the silence, the magic twirls,
A dance of the fates, where adventure unfurls.
With every heartbeat, the rhythm flows,
A timeless tale that forever grows.

So lose yourself in the foliate's song,
For enchantment here can do no wrong.
In this realm of wonder, believe and see,
The magic of life, wild and free.

Fluttering Souls Amidst Wistful Winds

With wings unfurled, souls take flight,
Chasing the starlight, embracing the night.
In the gentle breeze, they sway and spin,
Finding their place as the darkness begins.

Wistful winds carry tales once told,
Of love and loss, both tender and bold.
Through the valleys, they whisper and weave,
A tapestry rich, in which we believe.

The echoes of laughter, the sighs of the past,
Flutter like butterflies, hoping to last.
In the embrace of the twilight's gleam,
They dance on the edges of every dream.

So let your heart soar, lift it high,
For in the dance of the winds, we can fly.
With spirits entwined, forever and more,
In the canvas of night, our souls will soar.

Thus, the fluttering whispers call us near,
To share in the magic, to banish the fear.
For amidst wistful winds, we find our way,
In the beauty of life, we choose to stay.

Woven Threads of Green and Gold

In the glade where sunlight weaves,
Golden strands through whispering leaves.
Tender roots in emerald dance,
Nature twirls in sunlit trance.

Beneath the boughs, secrets unfold,
Stories shared in hues of gold.
Crickets sing in evening's glow,
Life's brief journey, soft and slow.

Among the ferns, shadows play,
Dancing light, twinkling ray.
Woven threads of green and gold,
In the heart, their tales are told.

Child of earth, beneath the sky,
Brush of wind, a gentle sigh.
We follow paths where echoes call,
In this realm, we rise and fall.

With every breath, the wild blooms sway,
Gathering dreams of yesterday.
In silence, we find our role,
Woven threads make us whole.

The Palette of Nature's Secrets

Brush in hand, the artist's quest,
To reveal the vibrant crest.
Colors blend from soil and stone,
Nature's whispers, softly grown.

Shadows dance on petals bright,
Every hue a stolen light.
The palette speaks in whispers low,
Secrets only dreamers know.

Clouds above in shades of gray,
Paint the dusk, then fade away.
In this canvas, hearts entwine,
Nature's beauty, pure design.

Rustling leaves, a songbird's call,
Ink of twilight, joy for all.
Each stroke a moment, bold and true,
The secrets shared between me and you.

In the silence, colors blend,
Framed by the trees, they never end.
The palette holds a timeless grace,
Nature's heartbeat, a warm embrace.

Reflecting Pools of Decomposing Star

In quiet woods where shadows lie,
Reflecting pools beneath the sky.
Memories drift like fallen leaves,
In layers where each echo grieves.

Stars once bright now fade away,
In the dusk where spirits play.
Water whispers tales divine,
Decomposing, yet they shine.

Pebbles gather, stories told,
Of shimmering nights in the cold.
Each ripple sings of time's soft flow,
The beauty found in letting go.

Glimmers flicker, hearts laid bare,
Mirrored skies reveal a prayer.
In these pools, peace will remain,
A cosmic dance of loss and gain.

Beneath the surface, dreams ignite,
Cascading down to endless night.
Reflecting pools, a celestial bar,
Where we find our own old star.

In the Embrace of Leafy Lullabies

Cradled in the tender green,
Nature hums a gentle scene.
In the crook of ancient trees,
Whispers sail upon the breeze.

Leaves embrace with soothing grace,
A lullaby in every place.
Silhouettes of life entwined,
In the hush, peace is defined.

Mossy carpets, soft and slow,
Where little hints of magic flow.
In slumber's arms, we find our way,
Dreams unfurl till break of day.

With every rustle, time does bend,
In leafy wraps, our souls transcend.
In nature's cradle, love complies,
In the embrace of leafy lullabies.

Let worries fade like morning mist,
For in this dream, we will persist.
Awake to find the world anew,
In harmony, we'll dance right through.

Veils of Memory in the Leafy Hush

In twilight's dance, the shadows weave,
Whispers of stories in leaves believe,
Echoes of laughter, soft and clear,
As time slips by, yet holds us near.

Beneath the boughs, where silence sighs,
Dreams linger sweet, beneath blue skies,
Each rustle tells of ages past,
In emerald realms, our hearts hold fast.

The path is worn by gentle tread,
Through wooded tales that softly spread,
With every step, the memories sing,
Of fleeting days and the joy they bring.

A tapestry of color bright,
In every beam, in every light,
The veils hang low, like gentle mist,
In leafy hush, they coalesce.

The essence of life, both old and new,
In dappled shade, in morning dew,
Within the grove, our souls entwine,
Veils of memory, forever shine.

Chronicles of the Leafy Ether

In the maze of trees, where secrets bloom,
Legends whisper in the gentle gloom,
Each bend in the path reveals a tale,
Of lost adventures, where dreams prevail.

A canopy woven with threads of gold,
Encircles hearts, both timid and bold,
With every breeze, a page unfurls,
Chronicles dance in the ether's swirls.

Beneath the arch of ancient boughs,
Time gleams softly in crinkled brows,
Each rustling leaf, a voice from yore,
Calling us to seek and explore.

The twilight gathers, a cloak of grace,
Shadows caress the forest's face,
In this retreat, our spirits soar,
Chronicles call, forevermore.

A lantern glimmers, in dusk's embrace,
Guiding us through this sacred space,
In leafy whispers, we find our way,
With echoes of laughter that softly stay.

Flickers of Sunlight Through Verdant Aisles

Through leafy aisles, where sunbeams play,
Dancing shadows in bright array,
The earth awakens with golden light,
In every corner, pure delight.

Flickers of warmth on a gentle breeze,
Swaying branches, rustling leaves,
Nature's chorus sings a tune,
In harmony beneath the moon.

Each step unfolds a secret kept,
In hidden glades where creatures slept,
A world of magic, alive and true,
In sunlight's dance, old and new.

Where blossoms bloom and dreams alight,
In vibrant hues, both bold and bright,
The heart takes flight, and worries cease,
In verdant aisles, we find our peace.

Flickers of sunlight as day departs,
Painting stories on eager hearts,
Graced by the touch of the twilight glow,
In this embrace, forever grow.

Adrift in the Whispering Grove

In the whispering grove, where secrets dwell,
Stories are woven, as time will tell,
With every rustle, a beckoning call,
As shadows waltz and the twilight falls.

Driftwood dreams on whispers glide,
In the heart of nature, we confide,
A soft embrace in the evening's breath,
Life's symphony, beyond sweet death.

Foliage whispers in breezy tones,
In this sanctuary, our hearts atone,
For lost hopes and wishes long deferred,
In the stillness, deep thoughts occurred.

Each flicker of starlight guides the way,
As night enfolds the end of day,
With every sigh, the darkness hums,
Adrift in peace, the spirit comes.

Within this grove, we're never alone,
The pulse of life, in every stone,
Adrift we wander, with thoughts profound,
In the whispering grove, true love is found.

Cosmic Hues in Ethereal Glades

In glades where fairies softly tread,
The cosmic hues paint dreams unsaid.
A whispering breeze through branches flows,
As starlit shadows dance in rows.

Beneath a velvet, swirling sky,
The moonlight weaves a lullaby.
With every twinkle, colors blend,
In harmony, the night doth send.

Each glimmer beckons, warm and bright,
A tapestry of pure delight.
In every leaf, in every glen,
A reminder of where magic's been.

The fireflies flit, a gentle guide,
Through realms where ancient secrets hide.
In cosmic dance, they swirl and shine,
Uniting heart and soul divine.

Ethereal glades, forever fair,
A sanctuary beyond compare.
With every breath, let wonder swell,
In cosmic hues, we weave our spell.

The Pulse of Nature's Veins

The pulse of nature beats so strong,
In rhythms where the wild belong.
A symphony in leaves and streams,
Echoing the world of dreams.

With every rustle, whispers call,
In shadows deep where echoes fall.
A brook hums sweet, as sunbeams wade,
Reviving life in every glade.

Roots entwined with ancient grace,
In sacred circles, time finds place.
The earth holds secrets, deep and wide,
In every pulse, the world's heart bides.

Crickets chirp their twilight tune,
Beneath the watchful eyes of moon.
In harmony, all creatures move,
Nature's song, a melody of love.

Summer blooms and autumn's gold,
In nature's saga, stories told.
As seasons shift, the pulse remains,
In every heart, the rhythm gains.

The Firefly's Serenade at Dusk

At dusk, the fireflies take their flight,
In shimmering dances, pure delight.
A serenade in amber glow,
They weave a tapestry below.

Soft whispers hum through twilight air,
As magic weaves with gentle care.
In fields aglow with fleeting light,
They beckon dreams to take their flight.

Among the flowers, shadows sway,
In flickering bursts, they greet the day.
With every flick, a secret shared,
In this embrace, no heart is scared.

As laughter echoes in the night,
The fireflies guide with loving light.
A dance of hope, a waltz of grace,
In dusk's embrace, they find their place.

With every glow, a wish is made,
In firefly's spark, our dreams conveyed.
As night unfolds in gentle sweep,
The serenade lulls all to sleep.

Chronicles of the Glistening Grove

In glistening groves where whispers dwell,
The chronicles of magic swell.
With every leaf that flutters near,
Stories linger, crystal clear.

Beneath the boughs, the shadows play,
In sunlight's kiss, they twine and sway.
The rustling pages of earth's own tome,
Reveal the wonders we call home.

Each creature holds a tale to spin,
Of ancient woods and where they've been.
A gathering of voices, strong and bright,
Together forming nature's might.

From whispered tales of long ago,
To dreams that in the moonlight glow.
The glistening grove, a sacred space,
Where every heartbeat finds its grace.

In every breeze, a story sways,
Of timeless love and endless days.
With open hearts, we heed the call,
In the grove's embrace, we find it all.

Twilight's Tapestry of Forest Dreams

In twilight's grasp, the shadows play,
As whispers weave through dusk's ballet.
The ancient oaks with secrets old,
Embrace the night, their stories told.

Stars sprinkle light on mossy ground,
Where echoes of forgotten sound.
The moon, a guardian in the sky,
Watches over dreams that softly sigh.

A silver stream, like liquid glass,
Reflects the past as moments pass.
Each ripple carries gentle lore,
Of restless hearts that yearn for more.

With fireflies dancing in the air,
They guide the night with fleeting flare.
As creatures stir in hidden glades,
The forest breathes in deep cascades.

Thus, wrapped in twilight's soothing shroud,
We wander lost, yet feel so proud.
For in this realm of dreamers' flight,
Our souls take wing, embracing night.

Beneath the Canopy's Breath

Beneath the canopy, shadows fall,
Where nature sings, answering the call.
Leaves rustle softly with every breeze,
Inviting whispers among the trees.

Sunbeams pierce through the emerald veil,
Creating patterns where fairies sail.
Mushrooms peek from the forest floor,
Guardians of secrets, tales to explore.

Rivers murmur their gentle rhyme,
Carving pathways through the sands of time.
With every ripple, a story spins,
Of life arising, and where it begins.

In twilight's glow, the creatures wake,
With the rustling leaves, a gentle quake.
Echoes of laughter, soft and light,
Draw us deeper into the night.

So wander here, let worries cease,
In this realm of enchantment and peace.
For in the whispers beneath each tree,
Lies the magic of what's meant to be.

Mystical Trails of the Verdant Realm

On mystical trails where shadows blend,
Footsteps echo, the magic won't end.
Fern and flower guide the roamers,
Through paths alive with whispered comers.

The air is thick with earthy scents,
Where every corner holds past events.
A brook sings softly, weaving dreams,
Of starlit skies and moonlit streams.

Birds weave melodies above our heads,
Their songs, like ribbons, in twilight spreads.
Each note a story, each call a part,
Of nature's symphony, a beating heart.

In hidden nooks, the wild things dwell,
Spinning their tales, casting their spell.
With gentle hands, we touch the ground,
And feel the magic that's all around.

So tread these trails, let wonder grow,
For every step, there's more to know.
In the verdant realm, let your spirit sway,
In harmony with the wild ballet.

The Lullaby of Descending Petals

As petals fall, a soft refrain,
The earth receives their gentle pain.
A lullaby for the weary soul,
Brings tender whispers, making us whole.

Crimson, gold, and hues of cream,
Each color tells a fragile dream.
The breeze carries their sweet embrace,
In this serene, enchanted space.

With twilight's kiss, they twirl and spin,
Falling softly, where dreams begin.
A carpet laid by nature's hand,
Inviting moments to softly stand.

So gather close and hear the sighs,
Of petals falling from painted skies.
In every drop, a tale withheld,
Waiting for hearts to be compelled.

Thus, let the petals softly land,
Marking journeys of the land.
For in their fall, the world will see,
The beauty in sweet destiny.

Fragments of Light in Shaded Lanes

In the quiet glade where shadows play,
Soft whispers dance, and spirits sway.
Moonlight drips through canopies high,
A secret world beneath the sky.

Gentle breezes carry a tune,
A melody sweet as night's silver moon.
The stars peer down with knowing eyes,
In this realm where enchantment lies.

Flickering lanterns light the path,
Casting aside the veil of wrath.
Each fragment glows, a tale untold,
Of dreams awakened and hearts bold.

From dusk till dawn, the magic lingers,
As shadows weave with light's soft fingers.
With every step, a spell is spun,
A dance of dusk, till the night's undone.

The Return of the Whispering Gale

When autumn leaves begin to fall,
And echoes breathe through silent hall.
The whispering gale returns once more,
To tell the tales of yesteryore.

In the hush of night, secrets rise,
Carried on winds through starry skies.
A soft refrain, a lover's sigh,
As shadows twirl and dreams comply.

With every gust, the past awakes,
Reviving hopes and cherished stakes.
An ancient song weaves ever tight,
The gale rejoices in the light.

When morning breaks, the echoes fade,
But whispers dwell in twilight's shade.
In hearts, the stories still remain,
Of love and loss intertwined with pain.

Tides of Time in Mossy Dreams

In the forest deep where time stands still,
Mossy dreams unfold with silent will.
Rippling streams reflect the sky,
As nature breathes a gentle sigh.

Among the ferns, the ancients speak,
Of fleeting moments, strong yet weak.
Each whisper soft, like water's flow,
Tides of time in a tranquil glow.

The sun dips low, a golden hue,
Casting a spell on every view.
As shadows lengthen, secrets gleam,
In the heart of every mossy dream.

Roots embrace the earth so tight,
Binding past and future in twilight.
Tales of yore, they intertwine,
Within each breath, the stars align.

Embers Ignite in Hidden Hollows

In the nooks of woods where whispers dwell,
Embers wait to tell their tale so well.
Flickering bright against the dark,
They spark anew, igniting a spark.

Beneath the boughs where secrets curl,
Life stirs gently in its quiet whirl.
The warmth of flame in shadows deep,
Awakens dreams that dare to leap.

When night enfolds with a velvet cloak,
The embers dance, the silence broke.
With every crackle, stories rise,
Of courage found in starlit skies.

In hidden hollows, magic breathes,
A celebration of forgotten leaves.
As dawn approaches, fires gleam,
An endless quest for every dream.

Mysteries Wrapped in Nature's Cloak

In morning mist where shadows play,
The secrets of the woods convey.
A whisper soft, a rustle fair,
Nature holds her wonders rare.

Beneath the boughs, where silence dwells,
The stories told, the magic swells.
Each leaf a tome, each stone a rhyme,
Wrapped in the veil of ancient time.

A flicker shows through tangled green,
As sunlight dances, bright and keen.
What creatures lurk in twilight's haze?
Awash in mystery's embrace.

In twilight's glow, the shadows blend,
Where every tale begins and ends.
A world apart yet just in reach,
Nature's secrets still to teach.

With every branch, a tale unfolds,
In whispers of the wise and old.
Mysteries weave through nature's thread,
A tapestry of life, unsaid.

Raindrops in the Heart of Canopy

In gentle sighs the raindrops fall,
A symphony from tree to hall.
The heart of canopy awakes,
With every drip, a magic breaks.

A shimmer bright on verdant leaves,
Each drop a gift that nature weaves.
The forest drinks in sweet delight,
While shadows dance from day to night.

From branch to ground, a rhythm flows,
A pulse of life where wonder grows.
In puddles deep, the secrets swirl,
Reflecting dreams of an unseen world.

Above the earth, a chorus hums,
As raindrops sing, the heart succumbs.
A melody of joy and grace,
In every drip, a warm embrace.

So let the rain, a treasure bear,
And quench the thirst of leaves laid bare.
For in this dance, a magic's spun,
In raindrops kissed by morning sun.

Dance of the Ferns in Moonlit Silence

In silence deep, where shadows glide,
The ferns in moonlit gardens bide.
They sway and swirl, a gentle dance,
In silver light, a mystic trance.

With every breeze, a secret shared,
The ferns respond, as if they're dared.
A flicker bright, the stars align,
As nature holds her breath in time.

Amongst the roots, the earth's embrace,
The ferns reveal their hidden grace.
In stillness wrapped, their beauty sings,
A hymn of hope on whispered wings.

The moon looks down, a watchful eye,
As ferns unfold and reach the sky.
In shadows cast, their stories bloom,
A dance of life amidst the gloom.

So linger here, where magic sways,
A world where night transforms the days.
In moonlit silence, let it be,
The dance of ferns, a mystery.

Veins of Life Amongst Timbered Whispers

In forests dense, where echoes ring,
The woodlands pulse with life in spring.
The veins of life, both strong and true,
In whispered tones, the secrets cue.

Between the trunks, where shadows weave,
Nature speaks to those who believe.
A rustle here, a call from there,
In timbered whispers, sweet and rare.

Beneath the bark, the stories dwell,
Of seasons past and spells they tell.
The trees, they hold the tales of yore,
A history wrapped, forevermore.

With every gust, the branches sway,
A testament to time's decay.
Yet life persists, as leaves confide,
Their fragile hopes, the dreams inside.

So roam the paths where whispers blend,
Amongst the trees, your heart to mend.
For in the woods, where silence dwells,
Are veins of life and woven spells.

Harmony of Earth, Sky, and Flame

In the cradle of dawn's gentle light,
Where shadows embrace a fading night,
The earth sings softly, a tender hum,
Inviting the dreams of tomorrow to come.

Sky drapes her arms in a silken hue,
Painting the world in vibrant blue,
While flames dance wildly, a flickering grace,
Binding the elements in a warm embrace.

Mountains whisper secrets, ancient and deep,
While rivers weave tales in their spirals and leaps,
Together as one, they weave their refrain,
A timeless symphony that conquers the plain.

Harmony flows through each rustling leaf,
In the heart of the wild, finding solace, relief,
Here earth meets sky, and in flame they unite,
A magical balance, a wondrous sight.

Beneath the stars, where the wild things sing,
Echoes of nature, a vibrant spring,
In the tapestry woven, where echoes belong,
Lives the harmony of earth, sky, and song.

The Whispering Woods and Fading Fire

In the twilight's hush, the woods softly sigh,
Whispers of ages through branches drift by,
Every rustle and croak, a tale to impart,
Sewing secrets of night to the day's gentle heart.

Fading firelight flickers, a warm, gentle glow,
Casting shadows that dance on the faces we know,
Gathered together, we bask in the cheer,
The echoes of laughter, the stories we hear.

Mistletoe hangs from the boughs overhead,
While owls share their wisdom on dreams to be fed,
In each whispered breeze, from the roots to the crown,
The woods sing of life and the tales woven down.

As darkness deepens, the stars start to peek,
The world breathes softly, tender and meek,
We follow the paths where silence can lead,
With the whispering woods, our spirits are freed.

Embers will smolder, yet still hearts will burn,
For the magic of woods waits for our return,
In the fading fire, together we find,
The warmth of the stories, entwined and aligned.

Chronicles of the Jaded Wilderness

In the heart of the wild, where shadows tread light,
Lies a jaded wilderness, cradled by night,
Each bough a witness to dawn's gentle grace,
Chronicles woven in time's soft embrace.

Ferns stretch and whisper, tales of the past,
Of creatures and wonders that seemingly last,
Where the wind stirs the leaves in a knowing sigh,
And echoes of those who have wandered by.

Amidst tangled undergrowth, stories unfold,
Of love and of losses, of fortunes untold,
Rivers carve journeys, relentless and bold,
Painting the canvas, a vision of gold.

Stars peer through branches, like curious eyes,
Observing the dreams that beneath them arise,
In the jaded expanse, where echoes abide,
Chronicles linger in nature's own stride.

So wanderer, listen to the soft-spoken air,
To the wilderness calls, tender and rare,
In every heartbeat, life's rhythm persists,
A saga of whispers, in shadows it twists.

A Mosaic of Green and Gold

In a tapestry woven from green and from gold,
Nature's rich palette, a story retold,
Beneath the bright boughs, a dance of delight,
Where sunlight and shadows engage in their fight.

Emerald patches with hints of soft hue,
Wildflowers peeking with colors anew,
Each stitch in the fabric a moment to hold,
A mosaic of life in the grandeur of bold.

As sunlight spills silver on petals that sway,
In harmony clutched, as night passes day,
Each breeze brings a laughter, a sigh from the trees,
Intriguing the air with all secrets it frees.

Dappled in shades from bright green to rich gold,
The earth spins its stories, both new and old,
With a heartbeat as steady as time in its flow,
Composing a symphony only we know.

So wander, dear friend, through the mosaic divine,
Where green and gold mingle, in nature's design,
For life is a canvas, we each paint our part,
In the colors of wonder, where dreams start to dart.

The Alchemy of Earth and Sky

In whispers of the ancient trees,
Where roots entwine, the earth agrees,
A dance of colors, clay and light,
Transforming day into the night.

Mossy carpets, soft and deep,
Guard secrets that the shadows keep,
While clouds above, in gowns of gray,
Shower rain in a silver ballet.

Golden grains in amber fields,
History within the harvest yields,
The sun dips low, a painter's sigh,
Brushing dreams across the sky.

Stone and star, a woven thread,
Linking lives, the love we've spread,
In silence, nature's song we find,
A harmony of heart and mind.

Oh, listen close to nature's tune,
From mountains high to valleys strewn,
In every breath, the world awakes,
The alchemy that never breaks.

Twilight's Lanterns in the Forest

As dusk descends, the shadows play,
A symphony of night and day,
The lanterns glow with soft embrace,
Leading us to a secret place.

Amidst the trees, the magic stirs,
In rustling leaves, a song occurs,
Each flicker tells a tale of old,
Of whispered dreams and nights of gold.

In twilight's arms, the stars appear,
Guiding wanderers, calm and near,
With every step, the forest sighs,
Beneath the watchful, winking skies.

The brook hums low, a soothing sound,
While fireflies flit and dance around,
Their tiny beacons, bright and bright,
Illuminate the heart of night.

And in this realm of gentle grace,
We find our home, our sacred space,
Together close in whispers shared,
In twilight's magic, deeply bared.

A Canvas of Shadows and Shimmers

Upon the ground, a canvas lies,
Painted soft by whispered sighs,
With shadows mingling, hues exchange,
A dance of light, forever strange.

The sun retreats, the moon ascends,
Where twilight's brush, soft light befriends,
In every corner, glimmers spark,
Illuminating the beckoning dark.

Colors mingle, undulating flow,
Creating wonders that softly glow,
Each step a mark, each breath a line,
In a tapestry that's truly divine.

As hours drift like whispers lost,
We celebrate what dreams have tossed,
Upon this earthy, artful page,
The heart writes on, despite the age.

So let us dance, in shadows dwell,
Embrace the stillness, cast the spell,
For life itself, a wondrous seam,
Threads together our love, our dream.

Time Paused in the Echoing Forest

In a grove where silence reigns,
Time unravels, breaks its chains,
Each leaf a note, each breeze a song,
Whispers echo, flowing strong.

Beneath the boughs, where shadows fold,
The heart of mystery gently unfolds,
Sunlight dapples the forest floor,
A timeless moment, forevermore.

The ancient roots hold stories tight,
Of bygone days and starlit nights,
In every rustle, a memory wakes,
Of paths we've walked and choices made.

Here, where time finds its sweet retreat,
Echoes linger, bittersweet,
With every breath, a heartbeat sways,
In nature's arms, we drift always.

So linger long, let worries cease,
In the forest's calm, you'll find your peace,
For time will pause, and dreams unfold,
In echoes of the stories told.

Serpentine Pathways Under Moonlight

Winding paths of glimmering dreams,
Beneath the veil of silver beams.
Whispers echo through the night,
Guided by the moon's soft light.

Trees sway gently, shadows dance,
In this place of mystic chance.
Footsteps fleeting, heartbeats race,
Lost within the quiet space.

Silvery mist wraps around,
Hushed secrets of the ground.
With each twist, a story's spun,
Of enchantments yet undone.

Glimmering lights, they beckon near,
Filling hearts with woven cheer.
Echoes of a bygone lore,
Guide the wanderers evermore.

Through the night eternal still,
Chasing dreams beyond the hill.
Pathways calling, soft and bright,
Serpentine in moonlit night.

Flickering Flames in Gloomy Groves

In the woods where shadows creep,
Flickering flames begin to leap.
Whispers of the winding trees,
Carry secrets on the breeze.

Glowing embers, hearts alight,
Chasing away the creeping night.
Imprints left on forest floor,
Tell of tales from days of yore.

Each flicker holds a story told,
In the warmth, the memories bold.
Crackling echoes fill the air,
Binding spirits with a prayer.

Through the gloom, the fires glow,
Illuminating paths below.
A gathering of souls and dreams,
In the light, the darkness screams.

Flickering flames unite the hearts,
In the woods where magic starts.
Gloomy groves, a hidden treasure,
In the night, we find our pleasure.

Mysteries Woven in Silver Dew

Mornings rise with whispers sweet,
Glistening dew beneath our feet.
Each droplet holds a tale profound,
In silver threads, secrets abound.

Gentle blooms wake from their sleep,
Guardians of the secrets they keep.
Nature's art in soft embrace,
Weaving magic through the space.

Glancing light on petals' grace,
Fragrant whispers time cannot erase.
Every twinkle, every sigh,
Calls forth dreams that wish to fly.

Beneath each leaf, a story waits,
In the stillness, fate debates.
Mysteries dance in morning's hue,
Woven tight in silver dew.

From dawn's embrace to midday's glow,
In the gardens, secrets flow.
Nature's canvas painted bright,
Holds the world in pure delight.

Dragon's Breath Among Starlit Leaves

In the whispering woods at night,
Dragons soar in gentle flight.
Stars like jewels, bright and clear,
Ignite the tales we long to hear.

Breath of fire, soft and warm,
Guiding spirits through the storm.
Among the leaves, a rustling sound,
Magic lingers all around.

Winged shadows cast their spell,
In this realm where wonders dwell.
Each flicker of the starlit scene,
Holds a promise, pure and keen.

In the silence of the night,
Hearts take flight, spirits light.
With each breath, the forest sighs,
As dragons dance beneath the skies.

Among the stars, they weave their fate,
In the forest, dreams create.
Dragon's breath, a timeless thread,
In starlit leaves, our hopes are fed.

Unraveling the Threads of Greenery

Amidst the ferns, the whispers weave,
Tales of sunlight and shadows leave,
Roots entwined in a gentle dance,
Nature's fabric, a mystic trance.

Emerald strands in a breezy sigh,
Climbing high to the azure sky,
Each leaf cradles a story shared,
In the tapestry, dreams laid bare.

Mossy carpets where secrets lay,
We tread lightly on ancient clay,
Trail of dew in the morning's glow,
A map of wonders we long to know.

Branches bend with a soft refrain,
Singing songs of the earth's domain,
Folk of forest, both fierce and kind,
In the weave of green, our hearts entwined.

With every step in this sacred place,
We find courage, we find grace,
For nature's threads never dull nor fray,
In the heart of greenery, we choose to stay.

The Tale of the Serpent's Trail

In the shadows where silence creaks,
A serpent glides, its secrets speak,
Scales shimmer with the moon's soft light,
A guardian of the breathless night.

Through tangled thickets and deep ravines,
It moves like a whisper in ancient scenes,
Each curl and twist holds a fable old,
Of treasures lost and love untold.

Beneath the gnarled roots, hidden and sly,
The serpent watches, with a knowing eye,
Legends crafted in silk and stone,
Echoes of magic, enchantment's throne.

With every rustle in the underbrush,
A heartbeat thunders, a shivering hush,
Threads of peril, a danger close,
Yet stories linger where willows dose.

What lies ahead, none can define,
Chasing shadows where the moonbeams shine,
The trail unfolds beneath the stars,
In each whispered tale, the magic jars.

Reflections in the Forest's Quiet

In hushed repose where shadows play,
The forest breathes, then drifts away,
Mirrored pools of tranquil grace,
Nature's canvas, a soft embrace.

Trees stand tall, their secrets hum,
As winds in whispers gently come,
Leaves converse in rustling tones,
A symphony of verdant drones.

Misty mornings, where echoes gleam,
Reflecting thoughts like a waking dream,
Silhouettes of past and present meet,
In rapture's spell, our hearts retreat.

Each footfall soft on the carpeted ground,
In this holy silence, solace found,
Nature writes in the language of peace,
A healing touch that will never cease.

In every pause, the world unwinds,
A thread of quiet for searching minds,
Through endless woods, we walk as one,
In reflections deep, the soul's true sun.

Litanies of the Leafy Plain

Upon the plains where green dreams lie,
Litanies rise to the open sky,
Leaves in chorus sing of the day,
Each note a promise that words convey.

Breezes brush with a tender hand,
Caressing softly this leafy land,
Whispers woven through stems and vines,
In nature's hymn, our heart aligns.

Dappled sunlight paints golden glows,
On petal-faces where sweet scent flows,
A meadow's laughter, a symphony bright,
Echoes of joy, under pale moonlight.

Here, the world surrenders its race,
To the stillness wrapped in nature's grace,
A tapestry spun from earth's own thread,
In leafy litanies, our spirits are led.

With every breeze, a prayer released,
In the open fields, our souls find peace,
In every leaf, a story lives on,
In litanies sung, we are never gone.

Gemstones of the Woodland Floor

Amidst the moss, where shadows play,
The gemstones glimmer, bright as day.
Each facet whispers tales of old,
In hues of green, and blue, and gold.

Beneath the boughs, a treasure lies,
The light of sun, it softly sighs.
A secret world that few can see,
Where nature speaks in mystery.

The crickets sing, the leaves they dance,
In woodland's heart, we find romance.
With every step, the earth reveals,
A magic spun from ancient wheels.

In twilight's hush, the colors gleam,
A silver mist, a fleeting dream.
The stones of lore, they call my name,
In every shade, a story's flame.

So wander deep, where wonders lie,
In forests vast beneath the sky.
For gemstones here, both wild and free,
Hold timeless charms for you and me.

Cascading Secrets of the Forest Glade

In dappled light, the waters flow,
Where secrets of the forest grow.
A gentle sound, like whispered prayer,
Invites the heart to linger there.

The ferns, they sway, in soft ballet,
While sunlight weaves through leaves at play.
A tapestry of green and gold,
A magic story yet untold.

The breezes carry tales of yore,
Of ancient spirits, and much more.
Each ripple holds a hidden truth,
Of laughter, love, and fleeting youth.

With every step, the glade transforms,
In harmony, the woodland warms.
The cascading sounds, a lullaby,
As echoes of the past drift by.

So let your spirit roam the glade,
Where beauty blossoms, never fade.
For in each turn, a truth we find,
Cascading secrets, hearts entwined.

Enchanted Fragments of Autumn Gold

The leaves turn shades of fiery hue,
In whispers soft, the winds renew.
A tapestry on woodland floor,
Where autumn's breath opens the door.

Among the trees, the whispers dance,
In fleeting moments, lost in trance.
Each fragment glimmers in the light,
A treasure found in day and night.

The acorns fall, a harvest cheer,
As nature sings of yesteryear.
The world transforms, a canvas bright,
In golden hues of pure delight.

With every step, a crunch, a crack,
The forest wears its autumn black.
The stirring air, both crisp and bold,
Awakens dreams of stories told.

So capture now this fleeting grace,
Let autumn's magic take its place.
In enchanted fragments, bold and true,
A wondrous realm awaits for you.

Murmurs in the Thicket's Embrace

In thicket deep, where shadows dwell,
The murmurs weave a mystic spell.
A chorus hums in gentle night,
As secrets stir in soft moonlight.

The rustling leaves, a tender sigh,
As nightingale sings to the sky.
Each heartbeat matches nature's tune,
Beneath the watchful eye of moon.

The thicket holds both calm and fear,
In whispered tales, so crystal clear.
With every branch, a story spins,
Of wild escapes, and hidden sins.

Yet in this dark, a warmth persists,
In every shadow, hope exists.
The murmurs dance with dreams aflight,
As peace envelops, soft and light.

So when you walk through thicket's home,
Listen close to the secrets roam.
For in the night, the heart will trace,
The murmurs found in nature's embrace.

The Heartbeat of Forgotten Woods

In shadows deep, the ancients sigh,
Where mossy stones and secrets lie.
The trees, they dance with whispers soft,
A symphony of memories aloft.

Beneath the boughs, old stories weave,
Of wanderers who dared believe.
In twilight's glow, their hopes take flight,
As stars ignite the velvet night.

A brook that babbles tales of yore,
Reflects the dreams of those before.
Each gnarled root, a brush of time,
In the forest's heart, a tranquil rhyme.

Through leafy veils, the creatures roam,
Each nook and cranny, they call home.
With every heartbeat, life entwines,
In whispered songs and sacred signs.

So wander here, beneath the sky,
Where past and present intertwine.
In forgotten woods, where magic stirs,
The heartbeat of the earth endures.

Chronicles in Amber Hues

In autumn's breath, the leaves do glow,
A tapestry of warm yellow.
As daylight wanes, the colors blaze,
In amber tones, the heart's ablaze.

Each fallen leaf, a story told,
Of quiet dreams and nights of gold.
They dance upon the whistling breeze,
In joyous waltz through ancient trees.

With every step on crunching ground,
New tales in whispers can be found.
The wind, it carries echoes clear,
Of laughter shared, of friendships dear.

As sunset paints the sky with fire,
We chase the light, our souls aspire.
In this brief glow, we find the muse,
In chronicles of amber hues.

So gather close, let hearts take flight,
Within the magic of the night.
For every shade that time endures,
Speaks softly in its glowing cures.

Ephemeral Whispers of the Verdant Realm

In meadows lush where wildflowers bloom,
The winds carry sweet perfume.
Ephemeral whispers beckon near,
Inviting all who choose to hear.

With every dawn, a fresh rebirth,
The verdant realm sings of its worth.
Sunbeams dance through leaves so bright,
Casting shadows, kissing light.

The brook hums low a serenade,
Of time's soft touch that will not fade.
Each petal holds a fleeting sigh,
A moment captured, then goodbye.

In glorious hues, the world unfolds,
A fleeting tale of warmth it holds.
In nature's grasp, we come alive,
In ephemeral whispers, we thrive.

So wander forth, let spirits soar,
In every corner, there's much more.
For in this land, where dreams collide,
The verdant realm, our hearts abide.

The Artistry of Nature's Erosion

With patient hands, the earth will shape,
Each rock and river, every cape.
The artistry of time and stone,
An unyielding beauty all its own.

From mountain high to valley low,
The silent sculptor's steady flow.
In whispers soft, the ages tell,
Of forces that both break and swell.

Through storms that howl and sun that blares,
The land reveals its hidden layers.
In scars and curves, the stories lay,
Each curve a dancer, swaying sway.

Nature's brush, with colors bold,
Paints landscapes rich, a sight to behold.
From jagged cliffs to smoothen shores,
The artistry of erosion pours.

So linger here, in awe and grace,
At nature's hand, an endless chase.
For in this realm, our hearts embrace,
The timeless craft, the earth's true face.

Whispers of the Verdant Veil

In a forest deep and wide,
Where ancient secrets softly bide,
The leaves converse in hushed delight,
Beneath the stars that weave the night.

A gentle breeze begins to stir,
As twinkling lights in branches purr,
While echoes of forgotten lore,
Call out from trees to shores of yore.

The ferns embrace the morning sun,
Where shadows play and sprites will run,
In every nook, a story spun,
Of magic frolic and pure fun.

A brook hums softly, sweet and clear,
With melodies that brush the ear,
It whispers tales of days gone by,
Where dreams take flight and hopes can fly.

In twilight's glow, the world transforms,
With shimmering mists—the spirit warms,
Each whispered wish a chance to see,
The verdant veil, a mystery.

Secrets of the Sylvan Mist

Beneath the arch of leafy grace,
Where shadows dance in silent space,
The mist entwines like tender threads,
Concealing paths where wonder treads.

An owl, wise keeper of the night,
Watches over with careful sight,
While distant calls of creatures sing,
Of twilight journeys on whispered wing.

The ferns unfurl with secrets rare,
In glades where fairies flit and stare,
They spin their tales in twilight's fold,
Of ancient magic softly told.

Crickets chirp a rhythmic tune,
While silver beams touch flowers' bloom,
In every breath, a spell is cast,
Of nature's wonders, unsurpassed.

As twilight weaves its gentle shroud,
The forest whispers, soft and proud,
In sylvan mist, the heart can soar,
Unlocking secrets forevermore.

Shadows Dance on Glistening Greens

In dappled light where shadows play,
The glistening greens come out to sway,
With laughter woven through the leaves,
Each fluttering heart a mystery weaves.

The sunbeams thread through branches high,
With golden strokes that paint the sky,
Each ripple through the emerald seas,
A symphony, the trees appease.

A gentle rustle, a creature darts,
In the compass of the woodland hearts,
With every sound, a story wakes,
Amidst the whispers that the forest makes.

The twilight glows, a meeting ground,
Where secrets gather all around,
The shadows dance with ethereal grace,
In every nook, a warm embrace.

Amongst the glades where magic streams,
The hidden paths, the wildest dreams,
In glistening greens, life holds its sway,
Forever in the forest's play.

Echoes of the Twilight Canopy

As twilight falls with a soft sigh,
The canopy is painted high,
With hues of gold and shades of blue,
In whispered tones, the night feels new.

The branches weave a tapestry,
Of mysteries that yearn to be,
And every star, a watchful eye,
That glimmers in the velvet sky.

From roots below to skies above,
The symphony of night they love,
The rustle of leaves, a soft refrain,
Echoes of magic in the lane.

A firefly dances, a fleeting spark,
Illuminating paths through the dark,
With every flicker, a path it shows,
Where dreams awaken and the heart knows.

In the twilight's embrace, the world can dream,
Of ancient lore and a moonlit gleam,
Each echo tells a tale anew,
Beneath the canopy, the night's debut.

Whispers of Verdant Twilight

In the glade, where shadows sway,
The leaves murmur secrets at close of day.
Moonlight weaves through branches tight,
Whispers dance in the cool twilight.

Gentle breezes stir the fawn's ear,
While crickets sing a tune so clear.
Nature's heart beats all around,
In this realm, pure magic is found.

Silhouettes merge in emerald hues,
As stars awaken, sprinkled like dew.
With each rustle, a tale unfolds,
In the tapestry of green, life molds.

A velvet dusk cloaks the day's end,
Where dreams take flight, and lovers blend.
In whispers, the forest calls me near,
In every breath, the twilight's cheer.

Here I dwell, in the tranquil vale,
Where every heart knows its own tale.
With dusk's embrace, we're intertwined,
In whispers of worlds, once aligned.

Shadows Dance on Embered Palms

In the glow of firelight's grace,
Shadows stretch in a wild chase.
Embers spark in the night so warm,
Dancing lightly, they twist and swarm.

With each flicker, a story bright,
Of lovers lost in the gentle night.
Memories cast upon the ground,
In quiet moments, laughter sounds.

The palms sway like spirits lost,
Treasures held, but not without cost.
Every shadow a lover's guise,
Every flame, a wish that flies.

Echoing laughter fills the air,
As night whispers softly, yet bare.
The warmth of dusk fades like a sigh,
And a wistful tear comes to each eye.

This canvas bright, though fleeting still,
Etches the heart, a haunting thrill.
For in the dance of shadows' play,
We find ourselves, lost and astray.

Echoes of a Serpent's Breath

In the stillness, a shadow creeps,
Where silence wraps and softly keeps.
Serpents slither with whispers low,
In the echoes of a breath, we go.

Every coil recounts a tale,
Of winding paths that twist and pale.
Beneath the moon's silver sheen,
Secrets linger in places unseen.

Eyes like lanterns, bright and wise,
Glimmer softly with no disguise.
The forest listens, holds its breath,
In the dance of life and whispered death.

Winds carry stories through the trees,
A requiem sung by the gentle breeze.
From roots to canopy, tales are spun,
In shadows cast, we all are one.

As night cools over the ancient ground,
In serpent's breath, wisdom is found.
Weaving fate with each silent sigh,
In the echoes of night, dreams lie.

The Sigh of Timeless Canopies

Beneath the arch of branches wide,
Ancient stories in shadows bide.
Whispers of time in rustling leaves,
The canopy sighs, the heart believes.

In golden light that pierces through,
Life unfolds with each morning dew.
Glimmers of sunlight play and glide,
Amidst the boughs where dreams reside.

With roots that delve in history's art,
The trees embrace with a knowing heart.
In the shade, we find our place,
In timeless evenings, we trace our grace.

Season's change in colors bright,
From verdant greens to winter's white.
Each sigh speaks of what's once seen,
In the stillness, where we have been.

So let us dwell in nature's breath,
In sacred spaces, we're absolved of death.
Embraced by canopies, both warm and wide,
In the sighs of time, may we forever hide.

Constellations Wrapped in Curls of Smoke

In twilight's grasp, the stars align,
With whispers soft, they weave and twine.
A tapestry of dreams takes flight,
In curls of smoke, they dance through night.

Each spark, a wish upon the breeze,
A flickered light among the trees.
They shimmer bright, then fade away,
As shadows stretch to greet the day.

Through swirling mist, a story's spun,
Of ancient dreams and battles won.
In every sigh, a tale unfolds,
Of magic lost and secrets told.

With every breath, the cosmos sighs,
As slumber's spell draws nigh,
In curls of smoke, the stars unite,
To guide us through the velvet night.

So when you gaze at skies above,
Remember well the stars you love.
In constellations wrapped in dreams,
The world is more than what it seems.

The Dance of Dreams Beneath the Horizon

In twilight's hush, dreams gently play,
Beneath the horizon, night meets day.
With every flutter, shadows sway,
In magical steps, they find their way.

As moonlight spills like silver threads,
It weaves through thoughts, where hope still spreads.
With every heartbeat, a promise gleams,
A whispered wish, a tapestry of dreams.

Stars join in, a glowing ballet,
Their twinkling lights a bright array.
Yet with each glance, they start to fade,
Like fleeting echoes of a softly played.

The horizon blurs, where realms entwine,
In this sacred space, your heart will shine.
For every dream beneath the sky,
Is a step away from a quiet sigh.

So let them dance, those dreams of yours,
In the vast expanse where magic soars.
At dawn, they fade, yet in our soul,
They linger on, to make us whole.

Flickers of Magic in the Underbrush

In shadowed glades, where whispers dwell,
Flickers of magic weave a spell.
Through emerald leaves, a laughter stirs,
As tiny wonders hum and purr.

Beneath the boughs, they dart and flit,
A world unseen, where fairies sit.
With every breath, a secret found,
In underbrush, where spells abound.

Soft glimmers dance, refracting light,
A symphony of colors bright.
In hidden nooks, such sweet delight,
Awaits the curious, poised for flight.

Among the ferns, in twilight's embrace,
Magic blooms, a sacred space.
A flicker here, a flutter there,
In silent moments, dreams declare.

So linger long in nature's yard,
Where wonder waits, though paths be hard.
For in the brush, where secrets sigh,
Flickers of magic never die.

Nightfall's Kiss on Sylvan Dreams

As day gives way to velvet skies,
Nightfall's kiss brings calm replies.
The forest sighs, a gentle sweep,
Where sylvan dreams begin to creep.

The stars alight, like lanterns bright,
In shadows deep, they spark delight.
With every breath, the night unveils,
A world where magic never fails.

In whispered winds, we hear their song,
Of ancient tales where we belong.
With every glance, the heart will sway,
As night enfolds the fading day.

In dappled light, where secrets hide,
We stroll through dreams, side by side.
With nightfall's kiss, the soul takes flight,
Exploring realms of endless night.

So journey on through moonlit streams,
Embrace the magic in your dreams.
For every kiss that night bestows,
Awakens hope as twilight glows.